BRING THE
OUTSIDE IN

THE ESSENTIAL GUIDE TO CACTI, SUCCULENTS, PLANTERS AND TERRARIUMS

VAL BRADLEY

BANTAM PRESS

LONDON · TORONTO · SYDNEY · AUCKLAND · JOHANNESBURG

INTRODUCTION

Why have plants in your home? Because they give it personality and make your space unique? Because they put you in touch with the living world? Because research has shown that having plants around you improves your mood? Or just because you like them!

This book will tell you everything you need to know about displaying plants at home, from growing pretty flowering plants that enhance well-being, to creating an attractive table-top terrarium, or planting dramatic foliage that makes a statement. Whether you prefer a hanging, free-standing or trailing plant – something edible or just ornamental – this book has all the information you need to get started.

CONTENTS

COOL & SHADY
CLOSED TERRARIUM

An enclosed glass container means that moisture given off by the plants condenses and is recycled to keep them growing.

YOU NEED
———

CLEAR GLASS CONTAINER

• • •

GRAVEL

• • •

COMPOST

• • •

PLANTS

CHOOSE YOUR PLANTS
———

Look for small leafy plants that love moisture and will still fit inside the container as they grow.

EXAMPLES: *Ferns, Ficus pumila, Hypoestes, Selaginella.*

WHAT KIND OF CONTAINER?
———

Any clear glass container with a tight-fitting lid will work as long as the sides and base are waterproof.

HOW TO DO IT

1
...
Put a layer of gravel in the base of the container and add a layer of compost.

2
...
Remove the pots and position the plant(s).

3
...
Mist gently to settle the compost, adding more compost if the roots show.

4
...
Once the compost is thoroughly moist, close the lid and keep it closed.

— MAKE IT HAPPY —
Put it near a non-sunny window.

— HOW LONG WILL IT LAST? —
If you keep it watered by misting it once a week and add a small quantity of liquid houseplant food once a month, it should last until the plants are too big for the container. They can then be put into larger pots.

DON'T

Don't put this kind of container in a sunny spot or the leaves will be damaged by sunlight through the glass.

...

Don't use plants that like dry conditions (cacti or succulents) or put plants with hairy leaves (e.g. African violet) in a humid container like this because they'll rot.

OPEN TERRARIUM

The sides of an open glass terrarium create a microclimate for the plants inside, trapping moisture around the leaves and reducing the need to water.

YOU NEED

CLEAR GLASS CONTAINER

• • •

GRAVEL

• • •

COMPOST

• • •

PLANTS

CHOOSE YOUR PLANTS

You need small, leafy plants that will fit inside the container as they grow.

EXAMPLES: *Elatostema, Ferns, Peperomia, Pilea.*

WHAT KIND OF CONTAINER?

Any glass container with high and/or incurving sides.

HOW TO DO IT

1
...
Arrange the plants in the container while still in their pots to make sure they fit.

2
...
Put layers of gravel and compost in your terrarium. Take the plants out of their pots.

3
...
Position the plants, adding compost around them as you go.

4
...
Water gently to settle them in.

— MAKE IT HAPPY —
Put it near a non-sunny window.

— HOW LONG WILL IT LAST? —
If you water it about once a week to make sure it doesn't dry out and add a small quantity of liquid houseplant food once a month, it should last until the plants are too big for the container.

DON'T
Don't put this kind of container in a really sunny spot or the leaves will be damaged by sunlight.

CACTUS COLLECTION

Cacti come from hot, dry areas, where they have adapted to the conditions by reducing their leaves to spines to conserve moisture. They are the ideal easy-care solution to a sunny windowsill where leafy plants would struggle. They grow slowly and – if they're happy – they'll produce colourful flowers.

YOU NEED

A SELECTION OF CONTAINERS

• • •

DECORATIVE GRAVEL

• • •

COMPOST

• • •

PLANTS

• • •

PIECE OF NEWSPAPER

CHOOSE YOUR PLANTS

You will need small cacti plants that will look attractive together. There are lots of different shapes available.

EXAMPLES: *Mammillaria, Parodia, Rebutia.*

WHAT KIND OF CONTAINER?

The aim is to create a collection of cacti, so choose containers that match or coordinate. You could put the cacti together in a single wide, shallow container and add angular stones to make a miniature landscape.

HOW TO DO IT

1
...
Put a layer of compost in the base of each pot.

2
...
Hold each plant with folded newspaper to protect your fingers as you position it.

3
...
Add compost up to the rim and press it down lightly to secure the plants in place. Use the blunt end of a pencil if you can't get your fingers in.

4
...
Cover the surface with a layer of decorative grit.

— MAKE IT HAPPY —

Put the plants near a sunny window.

— HOW LONG WILL IT LAST? —

Cacti can store water inside the plant, but they still need extra, especially if they're in a particularly hot spot. Water weekly and feed monthly from spring to autumn and then water once a month over the winter. If the plants start to look shrivelled and wrinkly, they *really* need watering. If you remember to check them regularly, they should last until the plants are too big for the containers.

Don't put your cacti in a dark corner or they will die.

...

Don't water cacti from overhead or the water droplets on the plants will magnify the sun's rays and scorch them.

SUCCULENT GARDEN

Succulents come from hot areas where the water supply is erratic. They have adapted to conserve moisture by storing it inside their leaves so they will be forgiving if you forget to water them sometimes. Unlike cacti, they usually have obvious leaves, rather than spines, and these have a waxy coating.

YOU NEED

CONTAINER(S)

• • •

COMPOST

• • •

PLANTS

CHOOSE YOUR PLANTS

Succulents come in all shapes and sizes, from the fast-growing money plant (*Crassula ovata*) to the tiny slow rosettes of *Echeveria*. Some flower, such as the *Aloes* and flaming Katy (*Kalanchoe*).

EXAMPLES: *Aloe, Crassula, Echeveria, Kalanchoe, Sedum, Senecio.*

WHAT KIND OF CONTAINER?

Work out whether you're going to grow a single plant or group several together, as this will affect your choice of pots. You might want to try making a circular wreath in a savarin mould.

HOW TO DO IT

1
· · ·
Put a layer of compost in the container and position the plants in their pots to create an attractive display.

2
· · ·
Remove the plants and put them in the same positions on your work surface.

3
· · ·
Remove the pots and add the plants.

4
· · ·
Fill the container with compost to the rim and water gently.

— MAKE IT HAPPY —
Place it near a sunny window. Water once a week from spring to autumn and feed every 4–6 weeks.

— HOW LONG WILL IT LAST? —
Succulents can store water, but they will need extra if they're in a particularly hot spot. Reduce the watering over winter to once a month and stop feeding them. If the plants start to look shrivelled, water them immediately. As long as you remember to check it regularly, this garden should last until the plants are too big for the container.

Don't water these plants from overhead. Instead, use a narrow spout to pour the water directly on the compost.

· · ·

Don't put succulents in a dark corner or they will struggle to survive.

UPRIGHT FLOWERS

There are two types of indoor flowering plants: those that flower beautifully for a short period and those that will grow and flower for years. You can choose an upright plant or one that can be trailed or grown on a frame.

YOU NEED

—

A CONTAINER LARGER THAN
THE ONE THE PLANT IS IN NOW

• • •

COMPOST

• • •

PLANT

CHOOSE YOUR PLANTS

—

There are many types of upright flowering plants and you can choose whatever you think will suit your room.

EXAMPLES: *Azalea, Begonia, Clivia, Hibiscus, Spathiphyllum.*

WHAT KIND OF CONTAINER?

—

Choose a container to suit your plant and the room where it will sit. Remember that many containers have drainage holes in the base and you may need to put the container on a saucer to catch excess water.

HOW TO DO IT

1
...
Ensure that the new container is a size bigger than the old pot. Remove the old pot (healthy roots are pale, fleshy and pest-free).

2
...
Put the plant in the new container and fill it up with compost.

3
...
Water the plant to settle the compost, adding more compost if you need to.

— MAKE IT HAPPY —
The peace lily likes a bright, non-sunny spot and is suitable for most areas, apart from over a radiator or in a direct draught from a door or window (which can damage the leaves). Standing the pot on a saucer of pebbles and filling this with water allows moisture to evaporate up around the leaves.

— DID YOU KNOW? —
Of the upright flowering plants, the peace lily (*Spathiphyllum*) is one of the best at absorbing the potentially harmful airborne chemicals given off by furnishings in the home and creating a fresher environment.

— HOW LONG WILL IT LAST? —
If you water your plant regularly and feed it with houseplant food once a month through the spring and summer, it should last for years. When roots start to grow out of the base of the container, it needs a larger one.

 Don't let your plant dry out.

COLOURFUL CLIMBERS

Climbing flowering plants can be grown upwards on a frame or can be left to trail down and soften the sharp edges of furniture. Some, such as Bougainvillea, are much more vigorous than others, so make sure you choose one that will suit your room.

YOU NEED

A LARGER CONTAINER THAN
THE ONE THE PLANT IS IN NOW

• • •

COMPOST

• • •

PLANT

CHOOSE YOUR PLANTS

There are some truly stunning flowering climbers; choose to suit your colour preference. Some, such as the different jasmines and the waxflower (*Hoya*), are highly perfumed and can be used instead of chemical air fresheners.

EXAMPLES: *Bougainvillea, Hoya, Jasminum, Mandevilla, Plumbago, Stephanotis.*

WHAT KIND OF CONTAINER?

Choose a container to complement your chosen plant and the room where it will live. Don't forget that many plant containers have drainage holes in the base.

HOW TO DO IT

1
...
Cover the drainage hole with newspaper if necessary (if there is no drainage hole, add a layer of gravel).

2
...
Position the plant in the pot and add compost to fill it to the rim.

3
...
Work out whether your plant will trail or climb on a frame and begin shaping it, tying it loosely if you need to.

4
...
Trim off any dead flowers or leaves and any shoots that just won't go the right way.

— MAKE IT HAPPY —
Check the label on the plant to see where it prefers to grow. Most flowering plants prefer a well-lit spot, away from intense midday summer sun (which can scorch the leaves).

Don't forget to water your plant or the flowers will die early. If you let it dry out when new buds are forming, they may drop off without opening.

— HOW LONG WILL IT LAST? —
If you look after it, it should last for years. Water at least once a week, especially when it's in full flower, from spring to autumn, and feed it once a month. Reduce the watering to once a fortnight in winter and stop feeding. Tie new shoots to the frame to keep them under control. You will need to repot if roots grow out of the base of the pot.

COLOURFUL CLIMBERS FLOWERING PLANTS

PATTERNS AND COLOURS

Foliage plants sometimes flower, but are grown mainly for their leaves. These may be large, well-shaped or patterned with different colours and the plant itself may be wide-spreading or upright.

YOU NEED

A LARGER CONTAINER THAN THE PLANT IS IN NOW

• • •

COMPOST

• • •

PLANT

CHOOSE YOUR PLANTS

Ferns are soft and pretty, palms are tall and architectural. The banana (*Musa*) and coconut (*Cocos*) are both suited to a warm, well-lit room, whereas spider plants (*Chlorophytum*) and *Fatsia* are happy in cooler conditions.

EXAMPLES: *Caladium, Chlorophytum, Chrysalidocarpus, Cocos, Codiaeum, Dracaena, Fatsia, Ficus, Fittonia, Maranta, Monstera, Nolina, Pilea, Radermachera, Sansevieria, Schefflera, Solenostemon.*

WHAT KIND OF CONTAINER?

Work out whether you're going to grow a single plant or group several together, as this will affect your choice of pots. You can choose from plastic, ceramic, metal or glass.

HOW TO DO IT

1
...
Choose your plant
and container.

2
...
Hold the pot steady while
you work, particularly if
it's an unusual shape.

3
...
Put the plant in the
container, fill it with
compost and water to
settle. Arrange the leaves
around the container.

— MAKE IT HAPPY —
Check the label to see where your plant
prefers to grow. Many foliage plants are
happy in a part-shady spot, away from
direct sunlight. As a general rule, the
darker the leaves, the more shade
the plant can tolerate.

— HOW LONG WILL IT LAST? —
If you water regularly and feed with
houseplant food every spring and
summer, it should last for years.
If it's happy, you'll need to repot it into
a larger container when roots grow
out of the base. Remember to water
hanging containers carefully to
avoid drips on furniture.

Don't let the plant sit in water or
dry out. Both overwatering and
underwatering result in brown,
dead areas on the tips or edges
of the leaves, which spoils the
overall look of the plant.

HANGING PLANTS

Trailing leafy plants are an ideal way to soften hard furniture corners and disguise plain walls. They bring an extra dimension to your plant arrangement and, if you have the space, act as a lush green foil behind colourful flowering plants.

YOU NEED

A LARGER CONTAINER THAN
THE ONE THE PLANT IS IN NOW

• • •

COMPOST

• • •

A SMALL SQUARE
OF NEWSPAPER

• • •

PLANT

CHOOSE YOUR PLANTS

Ivy (*Hedera*) and grape ivy (*Cissus rhombifolia*) can both grow quite long and need regular trimming, whereas the creeping fig (*Ficus pumila*) is small and compact. *Philodendron* supports itself using roots on the stem and is best grown partially against a mossy pole, rather than just trailing down.
EXAMPLES: *Cissus, Ficus pumila, Hedera, Philodendron, Syngonium, Tolmiea.*

WHAT KIND OF CONTAINER?

You can choose from plastic, ceramic, metal or glass to suit your plant and the room where it will sit, but remember that as the plant grows, it will gain weight and might start to overbalance if the pot is light.

HOW TO DO IT

1
...
Choose a hanging container and cover the drainage hole with newspaper.

2
...
Cover the newspaper with a layer of compost.

3
...
Position the plant towards the back of the container (so the leaves can come forward), fill it with compost to the rim and water to settle.

4
...
Arrange the foliage to create the best effect.

— MAKE IT HAPPY —

Check the label on the plant to see where it prefers to grow. Most foliage plants like a well-lit spot, away from intense midday sun, but there are exceptions. Ivy, in particular, is tolerant of most places around the home.

— HOW LONG WILL IT LAST? —

As long as you water and feed regularly, it should last for years. Water once a week from spring to autumn and feed monthly. Reduce watering to every 7–10 days in winter, and stop feeding. If it's happy, you'll need to repot it into a larger container once roots start to grow out of the base.

ORCHIDS

Orchids are exotic-looking plants that have intricate flowers in wonderful colours. Some are also highly fragrant, with scents of vanilla, chocolate and spice. Many orchids are quite easy to look after and the trick is to feed them well if you want them to flower a second time.

YOU NEED

CONTAINER

• • •

ORCHID COMPOST

• • •

PLANT

CHOOSE YOUR PLANTS

There are two types of orchid: those that live in the branches of trees and those that live on the ground. The ground-dwellers need a slightly shady, damp environment, whereas the tree-dwellers need light and air around their roots. It's easy to be seduced by flowers or fragrance, but try to choose one that will suit your home too.

EXAMPLES: *Dendrobium, Oncidium, Phalaenopsis, Vanda.*

— LOOKING AFTER AN ORCHID —

A new orchid should be happy in its container for up to a year, but then it will need a slightly larger pot if you want to keep it growing. Wait until the flowers finish before you repot.

WHAT KIND OF CONTAINER?

Tree-dwelling moth orchids (*Phalaenopsis*) need light around their roots, so they need clear containers. Ground-dwelling orchids don't mind the dark, so they can grow in conventional pots.

HOW TO DO IT

1
· · ·
Choose a
container a size
larger than the
one the plant is in.

2
· · ·
Take the plant
out of its pot and
shake it gently
to get rid of the
old compost.

3
· · ·
Put a layer of
orchid compost in
the container, put
in the orchid and
tap the sides of the
pot to shake the
compost down
towards the roots.

4
· · ·
Fill to the rim
with compost
and water lightly,
making sure you
don't water the
leaves, which can
make the plant rot.

— MAKE IT HAPPY —

Many orchids take in moisture
and food through their upper
aerial roots as well as the ones at
the base. They love humid air
in a well-lit (but not sunny) spot,
making them great plants for
the kitchen or bathroom.

— HOW LONG WILL IT LAST? —

Kept moist and well-fed, moth orchids
can last for years. Water once a week
from spring to autumn, misting twice
a week, especially if the room is dry
rather than steamy. Reduce the
watering to every 7–10 days in winter.
If overwatered, the leaves of a moth
orchid will start to turn black. To
encourage it to flower again, feed
regularly with orchid food (according
to the pack instructions) and move to
a cooler room for four weeks. If the
leaves turn yellow, feed it, and if they
become soft and wrinkly, water it.

BROMELIADS

This group of rosette-shaped tropical and sub-tropical plants, sometimes called air plants, take in water and food through their leaves as well as their roots. Some plants hold a reservoir of water in their centre.

YOU NEED
—

CONTAINER

• • •

PLANT

• • •

DECORATIVE BEADS OR GRAVEL

• • •

SMALL PIECE OF CORK BARK

• • •

2CM PIECE OF FLORIST TAPE
(OR STATIONER'S
ADHESIVE PUTTY)

CHOOSE YOUR PLANTS
—

Members of this group of plants naturally grow as epiphytes on the branches or trunks of trees, in rock crevices or on the ground. Their leaves can be quite leathery, but the flowers, when they appear, are brightly coloured.

EXAMPLES: *Aechmea, Ananas, Billbergia, Cryptanthus, Tillandsia, Vriesea.*

WHAT KIND OF CONTAINER?
—

A true air plant that has no roots, such as *Tillandsia ionantha*, can be planted on or in anything from a piece of stone or bark to a teacup. Plants that rely on their roots for stability, such as the urn plant (*Aechmea*) and pineapple (*Ananas*), need a deep container.

HOW TO DO IT

1
...
Choose your
plant, container
and decoration.

2
...
Attach the plant
to the piece
of bark with
adhesive tape
or putty.

3
...
Place the plant
inside the
container and add
decorative beads.

4
...
Mist your plant
regularly.

— MAKE THEM HAPPY —

Air plants live on atmospheric moisture,
but may need misting weekly if the air
is dry. When possible, they can be
submerged in rainwater and allowed to
dry. They like a well-lit spot, but may
scorch if you put them in full sun.

— HOW LONG WILL IT LAST? —

You can apply epiphyte fertiliser to boost
your air plant, but as long as you make
sure it never dries out (you'll know that
it's dry because the leaves will become
extra curly), it'll last a long time and
will gradually grow bigger.

GROW YOUR OWN FOOD

Nothing tastes as good as really fresh fruit, vegetables or herbs.
They haven't been treated, chilled or transported for miles and
are packed full of important vitamins and minerals.

CHOOSE YOUR PLANTS

As long as you have a well-lit windowsill,
you can grow your own herbs, tomatoes,
peppers, chillies, salad leaves and
microgreens. If you have a bit more
space and a very sunny spot, you can
grow a citrus plant and harvest your
own lemons, oranges or kumquats.

CHILLIES

Whether you prefer a mild chilli or
the intense burn of a Naga, there's
a chilli plant for everyone.

CITRUS PLANTS

With their glossy leaves, pretty fragrant
white flowers and tropical-looking fruit,
citrus plants are a fantastic way to
brighten up your home.

HERBS

Herbs are an essential part of cooking and
can make a meal taste particularly good.

MICROGREENS

Perfect for growing in a small space,
microgreens are ideal for adding
to salads.

GROWING CHILLIES

YOU NEED

A CONTAINER WITH
DRAINAGE HOLES

• • •

COMPOST

• • •

CHILLI PLANT

Bought chilli plants may have been grafted to join a tasty top to a strong root system to give you the best possible plant – these are a bit more expensive, but will give you more chillies to eat or store. Check the label, as it will state clearly if the plant has been grafted.

GROWING CITRUS PLANTS

YOU NEED

A LARGER CONTAINER THAN
THE ONE THE PLANT IS IN NOW

• • •

COMPOST

• • •

A SQUARE OF NEWSPAPER

• • •

CITRUS PLANT

Citrus plants do best in hot, sunny spots where other plants might struggle and, when they're happy, they can flower throughout the year. As it can take the fruit twelve months to mature, there are often flowers and fruit at various stages on the plant at the same time.

GROWING HERBS

YOU NEED

CONTAINER

• • •

COMPOST

• • •

HERB PLANT(S), SEED MATS,
SEED PODS OR LOOSE SEED

Soft herbs, such as basil and coriander, do better in smaller pots that you can use and replace. Woody herbs, such as rosemary and thyme, are stronger and longer-lived, so they need bigger, more ornamental pots.

GROWING MICROGREENS

YOU NEED

POTS OR TRAYS

• • •

COMPOST

• • •

A MICROGREENS KIT
OR PACK(S) OF SEEDS

Microgreens kits allow you to try your favourite vegetables at the tender, tasty seedling stage of growth. Some examples are chard, sweetcorn shoots, broccoli, beetroot, pea shoots, cabbage, watercress and rocket.

HOW TO DO IT CHILLIES

1
...
Choose a pot a size bigger than the current container and put a layer of compost in the bottom.

2
...
If the plant has been grafted, make sure the graft line (where the two plants join) is above the level of the compost.

3
...
If necessary, use a cane to provide support until the plant is stronger.

4
...
Make sure the compost covers the roots, then water gently.

— MAKE IT HAPPY —

Chillies do best in a warm, well-lit spot, but may scorch if they stand in direct midday summer sun.

— HOW LONG WILL IT LAST? —

As long as you water and feed regularly the plants should last all summer and may last indoors over the winter to give you a head start the following spring. Water every 3–4 days and add tomato food once a week. Reduce the watering to once a week during winter and stop feeding until the spring. Make sure you water regularly, as an erratic water supply can damage the fruits.

HOW TO DO IT CITRUS

1
...
Choose a container slightly larger than the current pot.

2
...
Lay a piece of newspaper in the base of the pot to cover the drainage hole, or add a layer of gravel if there is no hole.

3
...
Add a layer of compost and position the plant centrally.

4
...
Fill the container with compost so the old compost is covered, then water well to settle the compost.

— MAKE IT HAPPY —

Stand the plant in a sunny spot. Make sure you *never* prune a citrus plant too hard, because they store their food reserves in their leaves and if you remove these, the plant may die.

— HOW LONG WILL IT LAST? —

As long as you take care of the plant, it should be productive for many years. Water weekly from spring to autumn to keep the compost moist, and mist the foliage during hot weather. Feed with proprietary citrus food throughout the year (using both spring-summer and autumn-winter foods). Reduce the watering in winter to every 10–14 days, and make sure it is not exposed to frost.

HOW TO DO IT HERBS

1
...
Fill the container with
compost and tap the
sides to settle it.

2
...
There are three ways
to plant the seeds.

...
Take the seed pod and push
it down into the compost;

OR
...
lay the seed mat on the surface
of the compost, then cover with
about 1cm more compost;

OR
...
sprinkle seeds across the top of the
compost, then cover with about
1cm more compost.

3
...
Water gently and
place on a well-lit
windowsill.

— MAKE IT HAPPY —
Once the seeds germinate, stand
in a well-lit (but not sunny) position
and water regularly.

— HOW LONG WILL IT LAST? —
As long as you water them every
2–3 days and feed every two weeks
with houseplant food, the plants should
last for several weeks. Alternatively, you
could simply sow new pots every three
weeks to give you pot after pot of
fresh herbs to use in your cooking.

HOW TO DO IT MICROGREENS

1
...
Fill the base of the outer tray with water so it reaches the underside of the seed tray.

2
...
Place a piece of paper towel on the seed tray and sprinkle seeds generously but evenly over the surface.

3
...
You can sow a different type of seed on the other half of the tray, or leave it empty and sow half a tray one week and the other half 7–10 days later for a continuous crop.

4
...
Mist 3–4 times a day until the seedlings send roots down into the water underneath the seed tray.

— MAKE IT HAPPY —

Place on a well-lit, but not too sunny, windowsill, turning the tray round daily to stop the seedlings leaning towards the light. You can grow microgreens all year round, although they will take longer to germinate in winter.

— HOW LONG WILL IT LAST? —

Probably not very long! Harvest when the shoots are about 4cm tall or when the first true leaves appear after the initial seed leaves (about 16–21 days). You can make repeated sowings for a regular supply to cut, either using the same variety or mixing varieties within a pot or tray. Just be aware that they may grow at different rates.

GET IT RIGHT

BUY THE RIGHT COMPOST

Compost is so much more than the brown soil that goes into the pot around the roots. Plants take in food and water through their roots, and good compost allows this to happen, as well as allowing air to reach the roots and keeping the plant stable.

There are different types of compost for different purposes around the house and garden, but for most of the plants in this book, multi-purpose compost will do the job.

ORCHID COMPOST

Every enthusiast seems to have a recipe for orchid compost, but there are good ready-made products around. For moth orchids, the compost should have large, loose particles so that the roots get plenty of light.

WHEN TO WATER

There's no hard and fast rule for watering; it varies from plant to plant. Part of the fun of keeping plants is that, like pets, they have their own needs and you will get to know them.

Water according to the advice in each section. You can pick up the plant to gauge whether it needs any: if the pot feels heavy, it's full of water and probably doesn't need more yet (especially if water drips from the base); but if the pot feels light, water straight away.

THE BEST WAY TO WATER

Very few plants enjoy having wet leaves, because it serves no purpose and can lead to sun scorch or mould. It is better to water from below by filling the saucer the plant is standing on and letting it take up as much as it needs. Fill the saucer, wait 30 minutes and then check it. If the water has all gone, add more and check again. When water remains in the saucer, the compost is wet and you can tip away the surplus. Leaving a plant standing in water is asking for root rot.

Overwatering and underwatering

Both of these show as brown tips and edges to the leaves and/or wilting, so check the compost. If a plant dries out, resist the temptation to overwater to compensate: this causes even more problems by squashing all the air out of the compost.

If you discover that a plant is too wet, lie the pot on its side and leave it to drain for a few hours.

FEEDING

WHY DO PLANTS NEED FOOD?

Just like all living things, plants need food to survive. They use sunlight to manufacture sugars in the leaves, but they need to take in everything else through their roots in liquid form, using the water in the compost.

In the wild, if a plant runs short of food, it simply sends out new roots to search for more, but in a pot there's nowhere to go. The plant relies entirely on you to provide what it needs.

WHAT DOES A PLANT NEED?

The list of elements and minerals needed by each plant varies, but the essential three are nitrogen (N), phosphorus (P) and potassium (K).

Put simply, it's:
Nitrogen for shoots (and leaves)
Phosphorus for roots
Potassium for fruits

So if you're growing a leafy plant, it needs more nitrogen and if you want flowers or fruits, it needs potassium. These are shown on the plant food pack in a ratio of N:P:K so you can choose the right one. Most indoor plants are happy with a balanced houseplant food, but you can boost flowering by applying tomato fertiliser (high in potassium) at half strength as the buds appear.

CITRUS PLANTS

These plants need a lot of food to produce good fruit. Look for proprietary citrus food, which usually comes in two formulations: one for spring-summer use and the other for autumn-winter.

CHILLI PLANTS

Applying half strength tomato food once a week will help to increase the yield.

WHAT CAN GO WRONG?

You might think that plants inside the home are safe from the problems you find in the garden, such as pests and diseases – but when you open a window or door they're as susceptible as your favourite outdoor plants.

PESTS

Aphids (greenfly or blackfly): tiny insects on the soft tips of the shoots, on the stems or under the leaves where they suck the plant's sap. You might also notice the clear, sticky residue of their feeding, known as honeydew. Left untreated, the plant will become weak, with distorted shoots and damaged flowers.

Mealy bugs: these insects look like small white lumps on the stems and underneath the leaves where they suck sap. They will gradually weaken the plant.

Scale insects: small brown or green bumps on the stems and underneath the leaves. Their clear, sticky residue is also known as honeydew and you may notice this before you realise the insects are there.

Sciarid flies: tiny black flies that hover around the plants. They are harmless, but their larvae live in the compost and eat plant roots. They can kill a plant over time.

Red spider mites: tiny red mites that suck sap from soft shoot tips. You won't notice them, but you will see yellow mottling on the leaves and very fine webbing where they're feeding. They spread quickly from plant to plant.

DISEASES

Botrytis: known as grey mould, which describes it perfectly. It will attack young, soft seedlings and a plant that has a problem, especially when it is too wet. Good hygiene (clear away dead leaves and flowers), regular watering and good quality, sterile new compost will help you avoid it.

Sooty mould: this black mould appears on the surface of the leaf (especially of citrus plants) and will wash off – but it comes back. It lives on the honeydew produced by aphids or scale insects and won't go away until you cure the insect problem.

Rot: a general term for problems that affect plant roots, usually caused by overwatering or poor quality compost. You may see a plant wilting for no reason. Untreated rot will kill the entire root system. If you catch it in time, repotting the plant in sterile new compost and careful watering can help it recover.

———

Early identification and treatment are important for the health of all your plants, as problems can spread quite quickly.

———

TRANSWORLD PUBLISHERS
61–63 Uxbridge Road, London W5 5SA
www.penguin.co.uk

Transworld is part of the Penguin Random House
group of companies whose addresses can be found
at global.penguinrandomhouse.com

Penguin
Random House
UK

First published in Great Britain in 2016 by Bantam Press
an imprint of Transworld Publishers

A CIP catalogue record for this book
is available from the British Library.

ISBN 9780593078396

Location photography by Sarah Cuttle
Step-by-step photography by Chris Bradley
Designed and typeset by Smith & Gilmour Ltd
in 9.5/13pt Museo Slab
Printed and bound by Toppan Leefung

Penguin Random House is committed to a
sustainable future for our business, our readers
and our planet. This book is made from Forest
Stewardship Council® certified paper.

MIX
Paper from
responsible sources
FSC® C018179

1 3 5 7 9 10 8 6 4 2

— ACKNOWLEDGEMENTS —

The author wishes to thank Colin
Hambidge and Johnson's Seeds for
supplying the microgreens kits,
Catherine and Neil Wallsgrove of
Pepperpot Herbs for their superb plants,
Sarah Cuttle and Chris Bradley for the
brilliant photography, Joy the Store for
supplying the swiss cheese plant cushion
and Japanese bowls, Andy Allen and
Darcy Nicholson for sourcing the
additional props, and Anthropologie, Ikea,
Oliver Bonas, Next and Urban Outfitters
for their terrariums, planters and pots.
Thanks also to Susanna Wadeson and
Lizzy Goudsmit of Penguin Random
House for their imagination and
assistance and Smith & Gilmour for
design. Finally, thank you to Steve and
Nick Bradley for not complaining that
there were plants and containers
everywhere and again to Chris Bradley
for his invaluable patience and help
with this project.